Querida

Pitt Poetry Series

Terrance Hayes

Nancy Krygowski

Jeffrey McDaniel

Editors

Querida

Nathan Xavier Osorio

Published by the University of Pittsburgh Press, Pittsburgh, Pa., 15260

Copyright © 2024, Nathan Xavier Osorio

All rights reserved

Manufactured in the United States of America

Printed on acid-free paper

10 9 8 7 6 5 4 3 2 1

ISBN 13: 978-0-8229-4837-7

ISBN 10: 0-8229-4837-0

Cover art and design by Alex Wolfe, using Giovanni Battista Salvi da Sassoferratos's *The Virgin in Prayer* (ca. 1640–1650, oil on canvas, 29 × 23 in.) and elements via Adobe Stock.

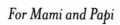

For Mami and Papi

Contents

I

II

III

I

That is why it breaks my heart, that game . . .
because after it had fostered again that most hungered-for illusion,
the game was meant to stop, and betray precisely what it promised.

—A. Bartlett Giamatti,
Major League Baseball Commissioner, 1988–1989

You can almost taste the pressure now . . .
There are 29,000 people in the ballpark,
and a million butterflies.

—Vin Scully,
Dodgers vs. Cubs, September 9, 1965

English as a Second Language

Surrendering to nausea in the felt-lined Tijuana-bound camper
I doubted the integrity of the breast-shaped nuclear reactors
fixed on the Pacific shore, cherry-pink nipples upright and beaconing
at a waltz tempo to the deepwater roughnecks swaying in their hemp
hammocks below a network of oil lines spouting flames into the oceanic
infinitude dyed dead-eagle-god red and I shrinking in importance

like in my collegiate days when I nodded submissively to a professor
who assured me my failure was because English was my second language
which is true if second to the cosmic mutterings of black holes
which is true nights I bellow desert monsoons into extinction
which is true when my hands are held up bearing the Atlantean
burden of brownness but which is most true here, surrendering

to nausea in the felt-lined Tijuana-bound camper
piloted by my dark-skinned father whom I've only ever understood in dialect
amalgamated from epazote and McDonald's fries gathered
between the San Gabriel Mountains and Popocatépetl
who continues his delicate lament of ash even when exposed
by the melting glaciers that once kept his mourning summit numb

I whisper to the Exxon™ Mobil gas station that I too can love
enough to become a volcano and reach out so that my palm
skates atop a gust of sea breeze and the invisible exhaust
of topless convertibles, blond hair pouring upward
from their front seats and strangling the open air uninhibited

and drunken with the riches of the west, the tall straw rippling
on the hillside in unison, the mega-outlet with its 24-hour security
desk illuminating the alleyways of the bad neighborhood
and the hordes of day laborers spilling out into the avenues
climbing atop trucks unsolicited, sharp-eyed and hungry
now I will say it, blessed be the Virgin Mary

that I've kept this close to the southern frontier
this close to the police beat and the ticking tear-gas canisters,
this close to the unidentifiable pots of spices roiling in the night markets
I reach to Gloria Anzaldúa and read *Borderlands*
till I lose sight of the swallows' nests that stipple the cliffsides
and drift onto the Harbor Freeway where in March 2006
the children of the frontier were in multitudes curdling traffic
a thousand strong as I sat sugar-buzzed and unobstructive in homeroom

and now my head rolls forward and I startle awake
the idle nuclear reactors pulsing longingly in the rearview mirror
the oil-rig plume billowing tenderly in response, our roughnecks'
night sweat cooled by the prospect of tomorrow's new depths
it baited as progress as self-preservation that will not include me
or my pilot or maybe even you, but whoever has and still sits
in the enormous leather chair.

The Last Town Before the Mojave

Hunker down, Heyzeuz, if that's your real name,
and look closely; do you remember us?
Gutter-born barrio, quiet patch of silt
populated by your benevolent
Río Bravo, her river roots cuddling
up near Coke caps and shredded beef dripping
from corn crushed flat. My advanced chemistry
lab partner wandered home last night howling,
Brother had nowhere to go but come back.
His jarhead still cut high and tight when he
hit the dirt, crushed glass and olive leaves rimmed
his wounds like a rotten margarita.
His body lit by the other shrine's glow,
Oh, how the San Gabriels still burn and snow.

Oh, how the San Gabriels still burn and snow!
Ash powdering the community pool
as Danny Trejo, our Patron Saint of
Pacoima, glares from his mural painted
on the east side of the tortería
on Van Nuys Blvd. My chulas with
their inch-thick eyeliner loiter beneath
and lament like mourning calaveras:
O Cempaxochitl! O Cempaxochitl!
Their thousand-spoked gold crowns blistering in
unison to the muffler two-step of
lowriders funeral marching to an
oldies dirge. Hot pistons popping skyward
to say, *You—keep your faith, all is fire.*

To say, *You—keep your faith, all is fire*
is to remember the horse's bruised knee,
the paved-over trails and the coyote
wearing the soda cup like a muzzle.
The brush fire smoked out all the burrows
and razed the thicket of jacarandas,
exposing the bent ribs of waterways
entrenched deep ages ago. My brother
lost his way home in our own desert,
dehydrated deer eye hanging from his
wrist for mal ojo. I am no longer
surprised when we stumble upon the graves:
the crack of smoldering trunk, numinous
wails, and then the silence of devotion.

Shelf Life

I count the stones I throw from the overpass,
its amber light buzzing in the fog that crawls

through the community college quad and over the quiet music
emporium, its dusty Stratocasters and sousaphones pointed proudly

toward the sun that will extinguish thousands
of years from now in a grand act of coming up short,

its spires of flame pirouetting into themselves, feeling whole
for the first time, a blues thick like the powdered malt

my tía pulls from the shelves of the warehouse club,
its display of oversized membership cards twirling on clear

noodles of nearly invisible twine above the cash registers
where Papi, with his head draped in a paper hairnet,

hands out hot dog and soft drink specials, his disposition industrial
like the tenacity of SPAM™ or the American spirit, his shelf life awful

and collapsing in a firework display of fear like our star,
the Sun, a name we've assigned to it to instill law

and order in the natural, in the giant of the uncontainable,
in the celestial passage of people from one place to another,

over volcano or desert or in a perpetually delayed bus,
its driver singing *The fare box is busted, oh! The fare box is busted,*

and continues to be on the urgency of avenues, numbered
to make sense of what comes before and what is to come after,

to fabricate anticipation and hope—is this why I'm convinced
of the end? Why I'm sitting in the early morning rumble of garbage

trucks and Dominican supers named Hank, contemplating the sun
on the first overcast day of fall, mourning the apple blossom

I haven't seen in nearly a decade or the family dreaming of wormholes,
Chinese takeout, and the warm embrace of ballistic missiles—

what a beautiful time it is to be alive! To shut down devices
and to think only of the plastic cogs in the hanging clock,

the filmy brine in the can of pork shoulder, and the five-pound hawk
who just last night I saw lurch to the center of the baseball diamond,

her plumed chest curdling time with each breath, her talons splattered
red with a pair of mice, her eyes amber and alive in the hills

I can see out my window, the space between the trees as black
as the marrow I suck from bones. I think one day I will retire

from this overcrowded town and head to wherever this hawk
has raised her family. There I will lie so that her nest

will eclipse the sun and rumors of war and its shadow
will find its home in my center.

How Hunger Was Invented

My knees bang against the pew with boredom,
not of God, but from hunger, a drowning
dream for the barrels of nacho cheese popped

open with a paint scalpel in the scalding asphalt
parking lot. The madrinas arrange a mosaic of
tables covered in the brilliant plastic of the 99

cent store. They know their devotion conjures
gardens of bounty in the 80-degree madrugada
like a desert oasis: springs of cherry Kool-Aid

and hazard orange contractor coolers overflowing
with champurada, Hot Cheeto bags cropped into
aluminum blossoms, and the hand-stitched servilletas

cloaking the capirotada and the conchas from the
salivating sun. Mercy! My bored knees thump against
the lacquered wood carved with "The Cool S" and

beat out a prayer for the divine bodies not in here,
but out there, beyond the confines of the tall ceiling
and the stained glass windows with their mournful

rendition of another, more significant, atrocity
against faith. In the sermon's second hour, there's a story
about a lone oryx wandering the Jurassic limestone

of a brutal land until Humbaba's jarrito of wine spills
out a red wave intoxicating it and me—O.K., you win.
I'm guilty of never having listened and as such will be

penanced to my rightful place at the end of the line,
to enter the garden only after all the chamoy chrysanthemums
have been plucked, muttering to myself seven Hail Marys

full of grace, sweating on the blacktop. Alone, I think of her
sorrowful gaze. The one that spears me from her altar
in the Frankincense corner of the transept. I carry such

heavy things long after the tables are collapsed, into
the longer days of boyhood: her starry cloak, the umber
of her skin, her belly, and the things it could have invented.

Earthquake Weather

My mother told me to never call her Mother
        but Mammmi, not Mamá or Mommy but
                Mammmi—emphasis on the mmm like delicious,

mmm like a masseuse pressing all her weight
        between your two worst vertebrae, the sudden pop
                yanking your breath from the shore of your lips

and into your throat. Or that's how I imagine it
        because Mammmi told me to never pay nobody
                to touch my body, not because of values, but because

they should pay you because you're worth it or
        maybe it was because she cut her hours at the grocery
                store to go to night school and bolillos in our brown bellies

were better than pain relief, better than knowing
        another stranger would be knocking at our door
                asking for their money back or for a small loan of quarters

for the bus like now, my neighbor's white body withering
        in my door frame from a mysterious disease. But Mammmi,
                for a moment let me be the honest one, if I had them,

I don't know if I'd share with someone who insisted you were
        my maid, which perhaps was an accident, but leaves me undone
                like thinking about your parent paying someone for touch

and dying men knocking at my door pleading for change.
       What I can hold onto for certain is that tomorrow I will wake
              to thunder shaking the walls of my suburban apartment,

and for a moment as brief as the arrival of light, I'll think
       I'm at my home in the barrio of dreams waking up to the Big One,
              to tremors ricocheting up the walls till the water-stained stucco

ceiling flakes off, blanketing my bedroom in asbestos.
       Mammmi, will you pound on my door and beg me to witness
              how the road back to Nicaragua splits open? How it shreds

the asphalt and unearths the condemned cemeteries
       from your childhood? The storm looms closer. The sound
              of thunder and lightning chasing one another

until they merge overhead, car alarms blaring in response,
       stirring the old dog till she rises blindly, dragging
              her hind legs across the carpet to realign herself

with the magnetic poles that calm her. In the end,
       her still wet nose pointed northward like a reminder
              that you too were once convinced that this way meant home,

that it meant you got to choose the way I'd remember your name.

The Mass Death of Mountains

San Gabriels, you are at my window hunching
over and dribbling finely ground granite from your lips.
I am sitting in this rocking chair, the one I found—

pulled all those years ago from a clump of garbage
outside the Beverly Hills McMansion I navigated to
with a two-dollar star map. I see bulldozers tidied up

in a neat row. I see their jaws shut like poppies
in the Mojave at night, shuttered in fields of wildflowers
you separate me from with their great horned owl foraging

in flight for an anonymous herbivore and its
soft-boned paws, incredibly pink in the celestial glow
of the Milky Way that I've only seen twice—

once in a textbook with an arrow labeling an arbitrary
coordinate with "You Are Here," and another time
when I pulled over to take a piss, my gaze expanding

as it slipped out over all the wisdom contained
in this cosmic gash peering into the past, more
or less like my ancestor must have once done,

her calf more defined than mine and still green
from the primordial pool she climbed out of, stunning
and vicious—all of this interrupting my half-sober drive

into Las Vegas, the spectacle of sound and color
slowly puncturing the desert vacuum on approach.
Do you adore me? I have loved you ever since

I first set my eyes on you while barreling across
the curving freeway overpass in a 1985 Chevy
Astro Van, a Cocker Spaniel pup with Hubba Bubba

matted onto his ears whining in my lap from car sickness,
Mami easing him with an oxtail bone
she had intended for the family soup.

It was then that I knew I had to scale your hillsides
with their abandoned merry-go-rounds, their stained glass
shot out by air pistols, past the apiary that I only knew

by the groan vibrating from within the underbrush,
until I arrived at the antenna farm that crowns your summit.
From these heights I celebrate all your vistas:

the Anheuser-Busch brewery and its forsaken amusement
park, the pandemonium of parrots that escaped
from the defunct sanctuary coexisting with the native

bats in murmurations, and farther off,
where the shimmering fringe marks the onset
of the sea, the flames of an oil rig no larger than what sprouts

from the Bic lighter held lit here in my palm,
the Santa Ana winds tugging at it, begging for an ember,
for more of that monthlong destruction that changes

the temperature of the earth, that still blackens the trunks
of the elder trees and the concrete helipads that rest beside
the missile silos hibernating in your back. How selfish

I turned out to be. I only came here to ignore the machinery
that reconstructs the face of your cliffs.
I claimed to be grateful, for all of you,

for your security, for the gaping horizon
you put an end to, for the home I no longer have to keep
warm with stove burners, but instead I rock here,

my thick serape swaddling my legs as I glance idly
out over your carved-out peaks and of course, dying too.

The Last Town Before the Mojave

Wails and the silence of devotion:
memories buried in the clenched-shut jaws
of the San Andreas fault line. They grind
and disturb the ash in the aqueduct,
our remains from an earlier fire
born from earth, wringing the gas pipes, crushing
open the hospital's veins, the toxic
plumes of Benadryl and blue latex gloves
evacuating above each of the
Saints' valleys: nuestra San Bernadino,
nuestra Santa Monica, nuestra San
Fernando. Their reddening crown is cooled
by starfall and the flurry of soot that
hoards the hallowed bones of a desert bat.

Hoard the hallowed bones of a desert bat
and scatter them at crossroads—this isn't
brujeria but hearing out your gut,
Abuelita offers as consejo.
I lift my eyes from my Gameboy, as it
pours a polyphonic spritz of 8-bit
beats across the kitchen counter into
the airwaves, the earned fanfare electric
when I rescue the blond green-eyed princess.
Abuelita braids her hair hand under
hand. Our ruckus does not overwhelm the
ritual of patience, the ritual
of batteries dying. The wisdom breaks
like the silent crash of inheritance.

Is the crash of inheritance silent
when the porcelain Virgin Mary falls
off the living room altar? Its plastic
tablecloth reflecting the glint of lights
hung from the shoulders of a thorn-crowned Christ.
His glazed eyes resting on the stitched horsehide
culprit, a commemorative baseball
rolling to a halt among chunks of shawl
and cheek. It casts a small planet's shadow
in the direction of the trinity,
three brothers, asthmatic from neighborhood
smog, glowing in home-run reverence, the
pitcher, catcher, and the guilty batter.

Welcome to the Show

I

I watch my brother fall asleep in the third inning
and wonder where the making of the game begins,
if it begins with the slow fill of the stadium and
its vast parking lots or with all the beer spilled in cars.

Their drivers showcasing honest fandom measured
in face paint and jerseys embroidered overseas.
Or perhaps the game begins before all of that, before
the kiss-cams and thousand lumen lights, before the hijinks:

the cylindrical beak of the Philly Phanatic deflecting
our eyes from the sweltering employee at his heating core.
Maybe it begins at the center of the green diamond
and its pasture, brilliant with dew in the quiet hours

of morning, where the immigrant mother heaves
the four-wheeled chalker across the Bandera Bermuda
grass to become an instrument for precision, transforming
space and time into the geometry that sets the stage

in motion. Her labor, the machinery that moves us all
from the bottom to the top of the inning, monastic
like the oil red beads of a rosary and faithful like an
old friend or the upswell of patriotism in an emergency,

in the tomahawk gesture of the Atlanta Braves
taken on in unison by thousands. Just like this:
like a communal act of violence, like the synchronized
crowing of that mother's son in the nosebleeds

and the family man with the season tickets
in a cruel ritual of assimilation. The chanting guttural,
devouring the alien crisp of October's air,
stirring my brother's exhausted head with revolutions

of breaking bats and the light pattering feet of anonymous
batboys and girls who lift the baseballs from the sandy warning
track to fork them over to the desperate children hungry
for more game, for more signs of life cracking from the bats

of their million-dollar heroes plucked from Cienfuegos,
Cuba, Culiacán, Mexico, from Incheon, South Korea
to be American All-Stars. Or perhaps the game doesn't
even begin in the stadium. Which now that I think

about it, reader, is an extraction site, like here in Los Angeles,
where the battle of Chavez Ravine was fought for ten years
till government promises for public housing razed
the neighborhoods of La Loma, Palo Verde, and Bishop,

cratering the Elysian Hills for diamond lust and American
sport, where the ghosts of Mexican childhoods
forever play in the haunted night of the city. The game,
if not here, must begin someplace further beyond

the offing of recent memory.

II

I inhale autumn and convince myself that the game
must begin in the awkward ache of adolescence,
in my high school parking lot before the fall classic
where the blond baseball jock, full of promise, flexes

to a ring of cheerleaders all done up with varsity jackets
and thick ribbons in their hair. The *As Seen on T.V.*
performance perfectly lit in the new blue of the streetlights
the city employees methodically installed by swapping each

of the burned-out bulbs for entire blocks, permanently
changing the color of the night, except in the public archive
and our collective dreams. You know how they say
we're in it together and that moments before a sudden death

you are alive—well, reader, I feel alive right now
and I do hope we are in it together, misremembering,
mis-reminiscing or whatever word we've made up
for that feeling of saying I went to that backseat to pretend

I was going to make love how they do in the vintage pornos
we found in the mouths of our parents' VCRs—
when really nothing happened. The new blue light
reaching through the tinted window of my lover's

2010 Volkswagen Beetle to find us imagining
the athlete and the blood it must take
to flex at the center of a ring of admirers.
Maybe in memory they're not there anymore,

but I swear to God, if I close my eyes, I can sense them all,
including the irony of those varsity jackets
thrown over their different colored shoulders like veils
or the beautiful synthetic threads of the home team uniform,

which makes us wonder what power we really have
when we misremember muscle or the post-game cruise
to the In-N-Out drive thru and its cashier whose braveness
equips her to reach into the lion's den of our sedan

to hand us a twenty-dollar order of animal fries and again,
dear reader, we must ask— which side of this civilian
war are we on? Can we ever come back from this moment?
As we embrace in the cradle of our backseat or from

within other great American landscapes like
the scorched topiaries of the ruined supermall
or the atrium of the slaveholder's university.
His revered casket another vacation destination

for our adolescent affection, the kind of affection that compels
us to these bleachers and maybe to a future cliffside
where we feast on the fleeting nuclear sun that swallows
the shadows and our flesh until we are perfectly alone.

III

During the seventh inning stretch, my brother wakes
to the sound of *Let me root, root, root for the DODGERS,*
if they don't win, it's a shame to ask me if I know
that Vin Scully was the first to call homeruns moonshots

and I look up, out from the pit of the stadium and
into to the sky to find nothing but the blaring flood lights
smothering the ghostly night I only remember in color;
its miraculous bruise black and red washed away

by the Friday Night Fireworks and American jubilation,
making it obvious that we are confined like water
in a well. Water, not glass-still, but riotous and revolving
in a wave caught in the hypnosis of our own clockwork,

of the progression of players whose atoms are electric
sprinting from base to base till they do their part
to return home, leaping into our arms
so we can embrace them high and proud,

as if they were our very own.

Overtime

I'm assured that on the devil's ridge
I'll understand my trek out from the valley.

I'm assured that from some vistas
you can still find the language in the fly's transit

across the orange sun. I'm assured that soon
my number will be up and that the butcher,

with the pink bloom on his white smock, will invite me
to begin to live, to undock my petite's damned ship,

which rolls in the harbor, the mystique of lies
gathering in a cloud of gnats over its tilted mast,

swirling to cover the sun in the smoky dawn.
Growl or no growl, I can't do this alone.

I can't bend myself into the knots demanded by industry,
into the forgetfulness that it takes to unhear the puma's cry,

into the dementia of time folding in on itself,
like a thick sludge poured into our hollowing cave.

Sweetheart, embrace me as l get old.
I can hardly hold the weight of it anymore.

How to Cook a Wolf

Probably one of the most private things in the world is an egg
until it is broken.
—M. F. K. Fisher

My mother fell in love with the way you cracked
into an urchin. How you kept the blade

    along its purple skull

      until it welcomed you

anxious to be separated for the first and last time.
Listen—from our window we can hear the Southern Pacific

    fume in the station. The turquoise room

      in the pleasure dome is only for the long-fingered

and bored, so come with me and climb onto the roof.
Sometimes, I remember best when I put my back to the warm
cinderblock,

    other times I have to reach my arm across your shoulder

      to find where you end. Darling, if you find me first

on the desert road I strung together with pins of light
or in the aqueduct blooming with graffiti,

this is where the sweet rot of leaves is coming from,

where the colony of urchins swarm beneath the dock,

where the twirling blades of the Black Hawk lift your hair.

We have been careful not to admit that we have wolves in parts of our home
we no longer visit. We have been careful to ignore the infinite snarling

of daytime, so come up for breath

and forgive me nights you can't sleep.

Yes, I will keep my ear to the floorboards and listen closely
for the sound of her parts assembling. Her lonesome days

are spent at the oceanfront,

the place where she drags out her dead.

I've brought you a canasta of strawberries,
the marble kind of gift from your childhood.

These things

have been outside your reach until now.

Ode to the Scallop

The scallop fits in the palm of your hand,
rubbed dry, pan seared until crusted,
an heirloom in gold in a heavy cast iron,
seasoned after each use in patient ritual.

The scallop catches a small leaf of parsley,
hides a glassy grain of sea salt, but before
then it's pulled from the soaked sand.
Water is to this shore what air is to our lungs.

There are flows of flows beneath the weight
of our feet and for a brief moment,
the history of this shore becomes our history,
becomes a record of our body and I am so pleased,

and maybe darling, so are you, that for a tally
of planetary time we are felt, embraced
by the wet of earth where I can't seem to find
the punchline, the gag where the tired clown

and her melted makeup breach through
the cosmic stillness of an empty stadium,
the stillness of being left in the rain.
For every scallop pulled up by galosh and rake

there is a choir more meditating with coral
and bivalve, meditating on all the sudden songs of earth.

It's Dark, but Not Late

I peel the tinfoil from our window
    to let the growl of the highway seep in.
        I see your reflection where the duct tape gives,

dimple proud
    you swallowed the clove of garlic
        to keep the vampires at bay.

You say when the snow comes you'll dream
    of ski camp giveaways
        and Nintendo 64,

but the anklet of bruises gives you away.
    You say we can't trust things that erase
        but we can relish the progress

of memory's gentle erosion.
    You point out the antennae field
        that pricks from the foothills

and insist that they are to blame
    for the firestorms of the century,
        for why the kitchen table

is more a pyre. Its fumes a perfume
    of cellophane choking the rooms
        where the children rested.

You swear you've never once seen
   the slot machines fail to light
      and insist on a deeper grave.

When we sleep talk about free lunch
   and Frito Pie Tuesdays, I remember
      the unpaved county road

where you would wait in the first light
   for the school bus, years before
      we ever met. Money has always been

an object and the garbage bag
   hanging from my neck
      is empty of its cold.

Come, Little Hunger

for Kristi

There are no bridges where I'm from because there are no bodies
of water and no living rivers to feed them except the chance arroyo
that after a sudden rain becomes a mudslide, which is not a mudslide
but a thick flow of debris. The contents of the channel, its splintered
baseball bats, scorched tires, the knotted crowns of zip ties and desert

willow, march in a liquid crawl against the stillness like the moment
the burrowing moth breaches your father's cotton shirt, which perfectly
remembers the contours of his shoulders and the things he held while
you waited for him on the outside. The possibility haunting like the hill
you saw ignite from your bedside moments before you laid to rest,

muscles stiff with the anticipation of slow destruction drumming up in
the Santa Ana winds at night. There are no bridges where I come from,
no rivers sprung from an ancient animal's mouth. Is the smoldering house
a sign of life or the lingering silence at the end of a phone call? Darling,
if I may, I've been told by people smarter than me that music puts out fire,

that the shower head doesn't carry all the voices you've ever heard, that
there are no rivers where I come from. If we stand perfectly still I am
certain our clasped hands can sever the debris flow, cleave the polyurethane
dinner set your mother abandoned to live in a van parked along a plunging
cliffside, splice the pages of the sports almanac from its tender spine,

ruin the electric money counter so we could see the machinery broken
for a change, and halve the fridge to see its hollow vacancy and how it shouts
the neighbor's hunger, her pleading with the Sheriff for one more good day.
His bulletproof vest nowhere as beautiful as the velvet green pods of the
Palo Verde who rolled its burls at the dark gray iron strapped to his hip

as if to insist that he was not fooling anyone, especially the desert shrub.
When all is said and done, can we turn into the bridge? So that the roadrunner
can go beyond the devil's fingers protruding from the mountainside, beyond
the tortured mineshaft that hoards the dutchman's gold, beyond the
shimmering fringe of casinos where I find you wandering shoeless between

the slot machines. Look, you've finally found a home where the cigarette girls
don't know your name. The poker dealer placard belonged to your grandmother.
I never knew Betty but I never knew your mother either, yet I can still hear
her small car idling in the garage that beautiful morning in Palm Springs
where you gave me a deck of cards and we fell silent, disappointed that

you never had someone teach you how to ante up. I want to lift the small
muscles of your body and lace the roadrunner between my fingers, the miracle
of its tom-toming heart against my thumb. There are no bridges where
we come from so you told me you can't remember where you pulled off
the highway to spread what was left of her. No bodies here, just the dust,

the bleached September sun, and the emptying arroyo. And yet after all this,
this is still not the bridge we were looking for but the infinite hot plates
at the buffet, the roiling water beneath, the biology of nourishment failing me
as it did you, and now I am telling you this: you are, after all, hunger,
the architecture of your skeleton, a prayer in the temple's furthest pew.

Flashover

We never make our way out
of the burning building
or from the rip current
that blinds us with sea
crystals as big as buffalo
nickels. No, no we stay
right here in the center
of the apartment, its contents
midair as if in the wings
of a typhoon. Your body divided
briefly by the barrel of Morton salt.
The Umbrella Girl catching
our stolen hibachi knife
in her arm. Both days of arson
and forgetfulness begin
the same, with your mouth
slightly open and the roaches
in the curtains and the pigeons
or palomas—we could never
quite agree—cooing on the
fire escape. Will you show
me your back again and
remind me which scars
are from puncture wounds
and which are from playing
with explosives? You assure me
that one day I'll pay for how

the darker waves began to foam,
for how I begged the pilot flame
to scurry out in the middle of the night
when the neighbors started hurling
beer bottles out their window
at the sewer rats feeding
on the carcass with a *licklicklick*.
This all seems so familiar,
the mildew on the shower curtain,
the hissing sound of being
marooned in the last stairwell
the rescue team forgets to search.
Do not pray for me. I was the reason
we undressed by stove light.

Empty Stadiums

Remember the baseball field,
how you got there so early
the crew still drinking their coffee
before slowly rolling away the tarp

to reveal the damp diamond.
You sat there as dawn
drained from the nosebleeds
illuminating, for the first time,

how you had thinned, how you had burnt
a new hole into your leather belt with the
red hot tip of a flat-head screwdriver
to feel more held in place.

Some of the insomnia was eased
by the highway that brought you
and by its perforated lanes appearing
before so easily disappearing,

by the car's rhythmic thumping
as you drove over the ceramic reflectors
to flirt with the iron guardrail.
The red and blue sirens splashed

the dashboard's hula girl
until it was nowhere as
voluptuous as you recalled.
But do you remember the floodlights?

The irony of their *what seems to be the problem?*
exposing the crack where years vanished
into another's night, into the furious
game of following somebody else home.

II

Querida, piensa en mí sólo un momento y ven
date cuenta de que el tiempo es cruel
y lo he pasado yo sin ti, oh, ven ya.

Querida, think of me just for a moment and come
realize how cruel time is
and I have spent it without you, oh, come now.

—Juan Gabriel

The Last Town Before the Mojave

The pitcher, catcher, and guilty batter
wake to the midnight fervor of summer,
to the synchronized howls of chained-up mutts
stirring the vacancy of the master
bedroom; brothers huddle in its doorway
to listen to the valley's nocturne break
into the fluttering of wings, into
the red hush of fear that diffuses slow
starlight, intoxicating the tangled
web of spiders. The magnitude of earth
exhales, fissuring the prehistoric
stillness of night. The riot surging through
mantle and bone, rupturing the boyish
impermanence of our memory.

Our impermanence of memory is
to blame for the trail of mud our soggy
Reeboks left on the kitchen tile, but
so is the thunderhead. It taunted us,
dared us to lie in the crabgrass until
its hull broke past the antenna field that
pricks from the mountain tops, and like proud sons
of thieves, we held our hard-fought ground despite
the warning booms that triggered car alarms
for miles, that warped the display case
at Blockbuster, that even gave pause to
the ring of the paletero's bells. So
if anyone dares to come ask, let them
know it was us. We drove out the thunder.

Know it was us. We drove out the thunder,
the earthquake and the roving hill fire
as we lay belly up in the silver
basin of the moon's empty ocean.
We anchored into its diamond dust with
handfuls of cempaxochitl harvested
from where the two parts of your mouth still meet.
Before we were children, we were the grain
that clung to the lulling sea of maize
you work so Mami can stay in love with
your sense of infinity—our heirloom
we discovered one midnight fervor of
summer at the heart of the changing earth
where she found us begging for your return.

Mami, Tell Me That Story Again

the one about kissing Papi for
the first time in the taco shop
on Florence, the one you would

take us to with the tiled fountain
at its center, the rusting pennies
in its basin growing mossy after

so many wishes. Tell me about
the scar tissue after the car accident
that crushed Papi's shin, how he was

an undocumented minor so the doctors
had no choice but to put him back
together. Tell me how public medicine

did a poor job of placing the long bolt
so shallow there's a color we can only
explain as a silverfish humming

beneath a veil of skin. You trace
your fingers over its threads to feel
how it remembers the winter's cold.

I can't remember where the accident
happened so that road has become
all roads. Oh, Mami, tell me that story

again where you tell us *we men*
can do better, where you're grateful
that medicine came at all to a boy

with no papers, and where you teach me
the inheritance of a furrowed brow
to keep the buzzards at bay. Yet even then,

the company pickpockets whittle
at his other bones until he's a bow
aching at the cash register. Mami,

did you ever kiss him there?

Self-Portrait as Papi

Papi loves to say *drink the beer, don't let it drink you*.
Papi works long hours at the grocery store, and if
I add the overtime, the holiday time-and-a-half,
the accrued sick days, and subtract the company luggage
gifted for thirty years of labor that he'll never use,
I wonder if he's ever left that place. However, for certain,

Papi is drunk in the backyard, tomato red despite
the bedrock ochre of his skin. In Los Angeles,
these are signs of drought, signs that even the roaring
wildfire can die from thirst but you couldn't tell here,
the slow gush of water reaching both the bush
with roses only slightly larger than his heart

and the sticky bin spilling over with crushed cans of Miller Lite,
an altar of aluminum. An open grave. Papi makes
beautiful things. But what can I make of the empty vessel
and its relationship to his heart? It's years later now,
and I have yet to gather the courage to name the thing,

despite the courage I spent summer afternoons collecting
bottle caps encrusted in the garden soil, despite the courage
of ritual, of unfurling his damp socks to witness his tomato red feet,
red like those roses, and still hot with the goliath distance
of his 12-hour shift at Food4Less. After a day at my desk,

I walk into my garden and unfurl my socks, lift my shirt over my
shoulders to reveal a blue softness, unbuckle my pants
until I'm left with myself. I don't need the control of reflection
to know the contours of my body, to know the stubborn ways I wear his.

Altarpiece

For the past twenty years, my days have begun in this warehouse,
with the only instant coffee I've ever needed or known.
The morning crew will want to talk sports to shake the sleep,
so I set the AM radio's dial to pick up last night's baseball score,
and I listen, my breath slowing to a curdle in the walk-in freezer.
They're always on time, swollen backs kept sewn together
by leather lifting belts. Once, I caught my son wearing mine
like a luchador. He pounded his chest as it hung off his hip,
yelling, *I am El Hijo del Santo!* Today, we will move hundreds
of cases of fruits and stack their bruised hearts
into miniature pyramids that tilt north, facing the sun
painted over the carnicería. I once thought I did good work
because it never ended, but now that I know that this sun
will not track against its painted sky, and that one day another
will come and lift the rolling gate to receive the next forty years,
I wonder.

—Papi

In the rearview mirror, I can see how the little one nods off
onto his brother's shoulder on the drive to school. I know it's 6 a.m.,
and at this hour, the fog gets wrangled in by the freeway and the hills,
but the walk is long and they're still too young to fold the towels
they dry their bodies with; the shower's steam
as thick as the mist now. It wasn't their choice to shatter
the porcelain Mary, yet sometimes, I swear, I can hear something
break when I shake them, asking, *What if tomorrow I die?*
like my mother once did. I don't tell them about how little I can see
in my dreams, how the earthquake opens up the road till it feeds itself,
stirring her photo locked in the file cabinet rooms away from the
family album. We pull up to the junior-high marquee
and before I can tell them to be good,
the big one opens the door, leads them out into the murk
until they're distant, and then gone.

—Mami

The tostilocos lady opens my Cheetos bag
and squirts hot sauce into it out of a red squeeze bottle.
A buck goes a lot farther on this side of the school gate.
Even time slips slower here, dripping from the olive leaves
that hang over the white and yellow shoots of grass.
The abuelitas in the park say that before the Spanish came
with their horses and the fat ticks sucking at their bellies,
this all used to be our land, but the gringa teachers don't talk
much about that, only the old folk I bow my head for.
I press my arms across my chest for their blessing.
Their hands, dark and wrinkled like an avocado, carve a cross
into the open air in front of me. I try not to get caught staring,
but I've heard that one of them has eyes the color
of rattlesnake skins we find in the hills behind our house.
They say if she does catch you, she'll sit at the foot of your bed
while you sleep and only disappear with the morning fog.

—Abi

What Do You Remember about the Earth?

after Bhanu Kapil

I do not remember the bending bough of the mango tree, the round bellies
of the fruit round like ours, round from the spools of tapeworms we found
in the outhouse.

I do not remember the long lake and the volcano at its center, the billowing
ash like a tower for the angelic, for lightning.

I do not remember the road that ran through the center of Niki Nomo
and the secrets it kept from the adults, the demon's procession in the early
hours of morning. The drunken hand on the doorknob, my five younger
sisters pretending to be asleep on the other side.

I do not remember the lumber yard and the photo of the shoeless children,
your aunts, humid among the splinters.

I do not remember all their names.

I do not remember the sweat stained man in the backyard.

I do not remember the howls of the monkeys fighting over a round bellied
mango.

I do not remember your grandmother and her beautiful hands, her thick
hair electric in the sticky night.

I do not remember the leftovers she'd walk home for her nine daughters
from the Italian restaurant she worked at as a waitress.

I do not remember your grandfather and the 18-wheeler he'd drive to haul lumber from Managua to Los Angeles.

I do not remember the family he started there in his ferocious hunt for a son.

I do not remember if he was there the morning the earth opened, the morning after which all that was left standing was the volcano and its tower of angels, its tower of furious red bolts.

I do not remember the drunken man in the taxi.

I do not remember if your grandmother felt pain.

I do not remember which loss came first.

I do not remember if when the earth swallowed the city it took time with it.

I do not remember if your grandfather ever came back for her body or if he left her spilled in the street.

I do not remember if the earth closed over her, embraced her for me, for my sisters, for even you.

I do not remember who drove the station wagon of orphans to Los Angeles.

I do not remember if we ever make it back.

Boys of Color

for Ruben

Brother, I found what we started looking for when we turned seven.
What we prayed for beneath quilt forts, what we thought knocked
from the inside of the glove box of the neighbor's burned-out truck;
it's what we always knew shook the cavity of the ram we unburied
from behind the abandoned tuberculosis ward, what sent us running
back down the side of the mountain. Do you remember him?

I think he's always known we'd find it because it reminds me of his hands.
The way they looked when he proudly assembled the IKEA furniture,
glue sealing the cuts he confided were from stacking the coarse bodies
of pineapples in a produce department built like a replica farm.
The ceiling's cartoon sun casting triangle beams of yellow over the spotless
corrugated tin roofs and crates of kiwis in an eternal daytime.

Brother, stay with me. A little longer like the other rays of lightning do.
The storm tore open when we gave up and the last time I saw you
you sat cross-legged at its gaping jaw, your AM/FM radio's antenna
pointed toward the gray, playing the Top 40 loop Papi heard as he swept
the early morning aisles, populated by the repeating grins of Orville
Redenbacher and the Sun-Maid Girl. It's years later now. I never thought

I'd find it here, underground and illuminated by my wind-up flashlight.
Its pale heart reverberating out from the tunnelways, its ancestral music
maddening our recycled blood. I was afraid I'd turn on you, pull out your
last gulp of air to make it mine. Together, we would have been spat back
into the flooding arroyo, blended into the clay by constricting snakes and
human muscle. Brother, when did it all go wrong?

13 More American Landscapes,
a View-Master Reel

White boys
and their pink-nosed
hunting dog

Six coyotes hanging
by their tails

U.S. flag flying over
Roswell, New Mexico

The Liberty Bell's fissure

All the buffalo ever shot
from moving trains

The exchanging crates
of bananas for ammunition

Signed studio photo
of Lucille Ball and the Latin Lover,
Desi Arnaz

The U.S.-Mexican border wall
puncturing the Pacific

Cleveland Indians' Chief Wahoo

Interior of No. 11 Factory,
Buick Automobile Plant,
Flint, Michigan

Country Living's
42 Easy Casserole Recipes
and a pine green fondue pot
fireside

The daily discarding
of bodies

A brown boy
and a pink-nosed
hunting dog

Desire Paths

Abi, I want to apologize for all the times I hurt you
But before my enumeration of furniture suplexes, of
Cruel hands gripping your nape, of hexes to your
Dinner plate, do you remember how you'd disappear?
Exiting, perhaps, through the carless garage to hike the
Full-winged forest you swore was hidden beyond the
Golden fringe of the chaparral. I didn't believe you then.
How could a place so far be so close? Even now, my
Instinct is to doubt that my little brother trailblazed and
Jackrabbited through the brush alone. It makes me dizzy.
Knowing full well the puma's hiss and the welts from
Low laying poison oak, you braved the odd hour of
Moonrise over freeways and sought out the Hercules
Nike Missile silos that honeycombed the mountains.
Ñoñoso is what they called me for shuddering at the
Ofrenda you found in the clearing and for not
Plundering the mineshafts with you or spelunking in
Quarries emptied by drought. You were just my little
Rusted figurine of Indiana Jones, bent out of shape and
Severe about your hustle. You vanished into the fever of a
Titanic quest for a place that would bring us together, an
Underworld you mapped by flashlight on our closet ceiling one
Velvet latchkey night when the open maw wolves, not really
Wolves, but coyotes approached, making us wish we were
X-Men and not boys. All we could do was whimper and
Yip in response to their hypnotic panting as they
Zeroed in on why we wandered into their realm.

Querida América

Querida América, my lonely days are over.
I ride the train upstate past the military academy
to sit in gazebos in the woods and listen to crickets
as they pelt the headstones. From here, I can see

the black body of the mountain and where it breaks
open into the milky way. The belly of the dead doe
churns with the passel of possums I bury beneath
my breast. Querida América, I remember your promise

and put my lips to the gas tank. I whisper a line
from "Bennie and the Jets," *We'll kill the fatted calf*
tonight so stick around, and the crypt rumbles,
birthing a phosphorescent Union Seventy-Six ball.

The moths gather and mold their cotton wings
along its body. You were such a good girl,
with your tiny feet like mango seeds. My mother
fell in love with your curly red hair and the way

you ate chocolate straight from the conveyor belt.
When she got sick, we found orange rinds
and the smell of grass clippings. Querida América,
the last train home has left. You hung my serrated

baby teeth in the pines, fed me government cheese
and cow tongue, asked me to listen to the obedient
winding of the river mill. I dozed and when I woke,
you had sliced away my tattoo of languageless gods,

and tied the possums, tail-to-paws, wearing them
like a necklace to show me you were listening.
Querida América, our lonely days are over.
Our railroad has wilted. Our river, rotted.

Our moths are only statuettes. Our orange ball has
flown away. Our teeth hang on the dead branches.
Our crickets have turned the tinsel into nests.
Our mother is still on the operating table.
Our memory keeps her smelling fresh.

The Last Town Before the Mojave

Mami found us begging for your return.
Our throats opened skyward and dry heaving
in ceremony to the ceaseless blue.
The blunt heat fracturing the radiance
of our skin, lineage blistering
into opal cysts. We have become numb,
hallucinating paradise in the
haze of history. In this light I can
read from the capillaries of slender
saplings that no one is coming,
and although we have not remembered how
to collect the parts necessary for rain,
we nourish our bellies with impressions
of pyramids buried within mountains,
our bodies within specters and cacti.

Our bodies within specters and cacti
roam through the flood of smog that wells in the
valley overnight. My reddening land
smolders beneath a membrane of dust and
rivulets of sand tumble in a hush
from rootless hilltops, collecting into
totems at the feet of electrical
pylons piercing the atmospheric filth
and how rare do the wisteria seem?
Their incomprehensible lavender
captured in children's books sprawled before me
a place as distant as the illusion
of the promised land, of home, its fertile
soil as charred as the dreams I inherit.

Soil as charred as the dreams I inherit
cakes the pale knots of roots that dangle from
the center of his palm and into the
celebration of Saturday at ten,
the age when he revealed to me the heart
of the dandelion and what it took
to take back what was ours from the few:
Hijo, hit them hard and hit them again
and again, the broad spear of his shovel
plunging into the desiccated flesh
of earth. Each hunt for a vein of moisture
maddening, kicking up dust, echoing
the thunderhead's bellow as it summons
water, the dark glimmer of a dead god.

Water, the dark glimmer of a dead god,
bubbles up from behind the corner Shell
and seeps over the sidewalk, puddling
near a gathering of taco trucks and palms,
while a third grader dips the stem of a
milk white carnation into a jar of
food dye, tinting the petals teal as they
pull the dark ink through the length of themselves,
instructing her how to use natural law
to assume the qualities of the earth,
how to listen closely to the ruins
of civilizations razed to folklore,
how to become the waterless rivers
and cindery hills and erupt in bloom.

The cindery hills erupted in bloom.
Forgive me—I saw how they opened up
like the spider's nest at the garden's edge,
how from the blast came an animal howl
and the train of ash barreling higher.
Relief came in warm snow, winged and clinging
beneath the palm's fans that once batted in
a surge of cold desert rain, riotous
and thick as uncut emeralds. I have
almost forgotten my dreams and wonder:
What will come from closing my eyes? The drought
will wane, the humidity will collect
on my brow, fattening until whole and
as potent as the first maize of spring.

Hunker down, Heyzeuz, if that's your real name,
watch how the San Gabriels burn and snow.
You said *Keep your faith* and that *all is fire,*
wails, and then then the silence of devotion,
but who hoards hallowed bones of desert bats?
Is the crash of inheritance silent?
The pitcher, catcher, and guilty batter,
despite impermanence of memory,
know it was you that drove out the thunder,
and who found us begging for your return,
for bodies within specters and cacti,
soil as charred as dreams we inherit,
water, the glimmer of a dead god,
the cindery hills erupting in bloom.

Hymn for the Last Town

I will die in Los Angeles during the first rainfall
in ages, on the day the cacaloxuchitl seeds decide to sprout,
on a day that comes to me often. I will die
in Los Angeles, and although now I am frightened,
that day will wash over me and cleanse me
of the damp stench of wild dog, my mouth full
of sand treaders and my ears that have welcomed
the bounty brought in by the briny tide, the black
opal of shells I have collected on these and those
shores and surely on a Tuesday—my favorite day
to set my shoulders to the devil, to expose the pale
of my neck to the palm trees and their long yellow sun.

Procession of Flies

The tongue remembers all kinds of things
like your name and the blood I ring out from it.
I lift the lid to find the sow's head;
its gaping mouth a cave where a muscle
had been pulled from its roots.
It says, *No, primo, you've got it all wrong,*
a butcher's fever isn't for gold
but for the long hours in darkness.
I fish out the bougainvillea petals from the aqueduct
and let the casinos slip away into daylight.
When we see the cassette's black ribbon
and how it strangles the roadside shrine,
you ask, *Hijo, do you think I could have been someone?*
your body tumbling miles down the road.

III

En ti, yo sigo.

—Papi

Abandonarium

In the green rooms of the Abandonarium.

Beautiful cage, asylum in.

Reckless urges to climb celestial trellises that may or may not

Have been there.

—Lucie Brock-Broido

I

The councilman commemorated the site of excavation
with the great wall of Los Angeles.
He paid the monsters for their day labor in expired coupons
and asked them all to promise to come back.

II

The spectacular thing about monsters are all the tunnels
they leave behind.
The spectacular thing about their red scales
are their red scales.
When I lifted the lid
      what I really found was darkness
      what I really found was the heft
of an empty cage.

III

The monster said the extraction site is a cauldron.
It arranges our belongings after we've gone missing,
after we're consumed in the desert's fugue.
It decides which things do not belong in its miniature
constellation, which things are best on display hanging
illuminated in the meat locker.

Ritual for Crossing

In the extraction site, I'm told of home,
that it's thousands of miles away,

a relic buried in another mountain top,
a strange song encoded in black rock,

a scent eradicated by invasive starlings.
I'll never run my finger over its ridge,

never pull the blossom of it deep
into the length of me para nunca escuchar

u oler el silencio profundo de un pasado en niebla.

Ritual for the Campesino

For this you'll need a crate of oranges sold from a parking lot. You might need to drive through the artichoke capital of the world and then the garlic capital and so forth. When you arrive, a man will walk up to you, his face covered with a bandana heavy with sweat and dust. In this well you'll find: the sweetest fruit, tidepools of quiet, of uncertainty, of music. I collect all these things. Gathering them in my pockets till they overflow into the gutters. The Roman letters bursting with failure at their seams.

The ghost of our past knocks on the front door at 3:00 a.m., clenching tools and weapons, the essential building blocks of hard labor. The letter attempts to grind memory into paper, failing us over and over. In this ritual, pray for fire at the center of the mineshaft.

Ritual for the Descent

At the bottom of this well you can find it all. Everything we have ever been looking for. It flashes open like an SOS, whimpers in a groan, in a yell, in a grito. Today, I am afraid. But perhaps not forever, perhaps things can improve once we sink to its bottom. The language is weak in the mouth of the well, in print, the margins are steel walls, a container of unpaid labor.

When we leap into the well, I ask the councilman what he thinks of my math, if I've calculated correctly, and he assures me that I've got it all wrong.

Ritual for the Shore

I'm drawn to the cave

                of the wound

the giant mine shaft   and its abandoned

                machinery

wherever I've awoken

                I can hear

                        its song

like how the cold   morning air

        lifts the sounds   of waves

de una playa lejana

              de una playa

                    en total oscuridad.

IV

The X marks loss. The complimentary grocery store calendar does not mark time
but what has gone missing. It opens its plumed maw and cries:
there's nothing here but a golden palm cupped to carry the weight of
EXTRACTION.
Drawn by the glow, I trespass into the mine and its eroding metal.

V

The councilman tries to convince me that
their testimony is slippery, that it changes all the time,
that they've written the perfect algorithm of deceit,
autofilling our mouths with stock images of desert
cages. It fits all our metrics and matches what the
census prophesized. The councilman says
he has seen this coming: the open wound is dead.
It won't even fester—here is its last whimper of light.

VI

EXTRACTION
                    is on the autopsy table
as a tiny, framed photo of an eye.
Hear how loud it is when it's fired.
                              It's just a narrow bridge. It's just a narrow bridge
where the monsters cross over.

Ritual for Erasure

The extraction site is an omission: an archive of fingers missing in the machinery, of aerosols in the lungs of the campesino. This extraction site is the underwater sewage coursing through the city, the dust storm roiling outside of Barstow, copy language, the bureaucracy of an email, the eyes sucked dry of all their attention, the military base, and its poisoned water.

This extraction site is an omission of that which could yet still cannot: the bruised phantom limbs and the prayer passed from mother to son. This extraction site is an omission. The omission of weaponry, ginger tools of secrecy, the underground muscle buried in debris and shrapnel, the student coaxed into the firing line, the mutt dragged by her collar into the ditch.

The festering extraction site draws in like the center of the universe, the riptide in the dawn hours, the center of the breathing giant, the molten core of the celestial object, the affect kept silent in a straight face, all the bodies ever kept in a metal cage. This extraction site is an altar, a cauldron, a constellation of motions, a collection of impossible objects, of affect swirling toward a great white room.

Ritual for the Implosion

If you hold it all in, you'll implode, not violently but slowly like the
wrought iron vessel sinking into the underwater canyon of a deep well.
The journey is a gradual decrescendo as the orchestra pit wails, its cellos
pulling on their long bows in unison. From these depths, you can't taste
salt, you can't hear the dizzying crush of your ears popping. On our way
down, I show you how in one hand I can hold an entire archive. It sparkles
in the snaking light that dices through the murky blue. In the other hand,
I hold a raw flank of flesh.

This is where the metaphor ends. Where I refuse to be complicit in any
more acts of violence. I was told to promise, to keep a secret, and instead,
I told my version of the truth. I told them what it feels like to hear your
mother sing for the first time. I told them what it feels like to learn her
real name and why the tongue recognizes its deformations like kin.

I anticipate I will say a lot of things like this from the bottom of the well.
Once I arrive, I will make so, so many wishes, and pray to anyone who will
listen. When the hull crashes into the obsidian trench, I'll throw my head
back, allow my tongue to become tentacle and crawl along the lapping
waves of memory.

Ritual for Extraction

In this grave, I grab an old rusted shovel Papi gave me.
I'll sing it again for those of you new to listening: in this grave,
I grab an old, rusted shovel Papi gave me. In this grave,

I pierce the obsidian floor with the shovel and carve out a hueco.
I recognize that this grave in the grave might collect water,
winter, the stars, and their snaking beams. En esta tumba hablo

una idioma bien quebrado, una tumba al inglés, al español, pero nunca
a las lenguas originales, las lenguas que cantan que no están mudas.
In this grave, I dig and I dig until I find the soft wooden box. I'm left with nothing

most mornings I spend at its side. Where is its light coming from?
Where is the sound in this grave? How far does it sink into the earth?
I keep reforming the grave, and its miniature graves, looking for the relief

of a body. I never meet the requirements.

Ritual for Aisle 9

I'm told that I'm most alive in the melody of the "Hispanic" food aisle,
the banners of cellophane wrappers gleaming as if to gritar
que en ellos puedo sentir el corazón turbulento de mis antepasados,
gritar que en ellos puedo sentir la mano callosa
de La Morena, de Abuelita, de mi padre que ritualmente trabaja los shelves.

Ritual for the Fig Wasp

The prospector says my practice is ultimately a failure. That the tools I'm using are all wrong, that I'm better off blanketed in silence. I sit to take a few pounds off my feet. I lift my arms to dance to a song Papi sang to Mami the day they met. I lift my arms to show you that from here I can embrace the sun.

I take out a pile of popsicle sticks from the 99-cent store that'll close in a week for the barrio's first and last organic grocery store. If I light them on fire, the smoke will shout emergency. It will send panic through the village out toward the megaplex with infinite screens turned on to the empty parking lots. The silver screens are turned on to an early memory of Papi telling me to muster up the courage to shake the rotting figs out of the wasp infested tree.

The tree is no longer there. Papi chopped it down and it took me a long while to forgive him, a long while to see past all the dust that replaced the moist soil where I used to bury my toes. When I was strong enough, he taught me how to cut down trees too, until the field was dry, alone, and barren. *Then and only then is when we dig!* he shouted out over the salt flats, his voice vibrating the faraway dunes.

The wasps' crinkled bodies roast in the oils of their own thoraxes. In this desert boneyard, collect all those that have ever stung you. Line them around you until you have no way out.

Ritual for Infrastructure

The iron wrought vessel doesn't crash. It doesn't disappear into the cloudy obsidian floor of the well, taking the lovers into the lie where they stay together. So many years later and the nightgown can stand on its own in a parking lot in Los Angeles. The other artifacts pulled from the well bob their heads in unison.

I look forward to the morning we can discuss how we feel like we're living someone else's life. The smell of leather and dusty dog fur caught in the museum vitrine. I don't think we can live with that. I don't think in this grave I can walk the dog down the center of the road, a confluence of pavement and storm drain, of ice and milk.

VII

I went four days alone without anyone noticing.
I woke up to the councilman throwing up
lightning bolts outside my window,
whittling bullets from gold, stories into bones.

VIII

I had my
morning
can of
rations
breathing is
combustion
a slow
controlled
burn
this site
is not a site
of honor
but a pile
of minerals
a pile of seeds
a pile of
well-cut
claws

IX

The geothermal vents flush out the monsters
with smokestacks three thousand feet in the air.
Those without wings come tumbling back down
to Earth. The pumpjacks bob their heads nodding
in favor of the oil fields before bursting into pillars of fire.
From the top you can see the great wall of Los Angeles
and how it glimmers like a chain of positive data.

X

The councilman goes door-to-door peeling off our electrodes.
He tells us to flatten ourselves on the hot freeway and to look out
onto the shower of meteorites, the shower of torn bodies. He points—

Look at how beautiful they've become.

Ritual for the Beloved

Dear Extraction Site Tourist,

Find the pieces in the garage, find them in the unopened boxes in the
pantry beneath the floorboards, in the walls, insulated with newspapers
from 1962. Tear them out of the ground and out of the walls and build your
altar. Do not build the altar with objects pulled from the riverbed. Find
your sisters and your brothers lying on the hot main street and yank them
up. Tease them about the impossibility of light, the impossibility of the hair
behind their ears.

Be disappointed when the pedal touches the footwell to no effect. Embrace
your sibling and tell them how they were the measure of your growth, how
it feels to know someone that mirrors your own memory. At dawn I can
hear the four chambers of the heart the loudest. Why not linger in the bed a
little longer? The stench from the dog crate makes its rounds and the puppy
nestles his nose in the crook of his legs.

I am at my best hungry and tired, overworked and begging for silence.
The cathode television mumbles something about futurity, about survival,
about the planets and their menacing rotations. It too is a performance, a
desire for movement and masquerade. In the script, we're named a carnival,
a wandering show of monstrosities. I wonder then if this is too much for
them, if we're more palatable a vacant hole, an abandoned mine.

Ritual for the Circuit

El circuito todavía está roto y las luces de la máquina expendedora
no longer illuminate the break room. If I exhale in digits,
submit the proper form to the councilman on time,
the Martian lander still courses through outer space,
while the grave remains cold, mientras mi abuela y todas
sus abuelas todavía pierden el camino a casa,
el camino celestial vibrando con una canción desconocida.

Ritual for the Latchkeys

The boys play a card game in the elementary school parking lot,
the sun at their shoulders, their skin darkening,
curing itself according to solar rhythms, to palpitations in the bones
of crow wings. At the day's end they lift their heads, fully understanding the gravity
of their location, *desde aquí entendemos todo. Poco a poco se lo quitarán.*

Ritual for Ruins

In the warehouse, el paletero rings his bells to an audience
of wooden planks and mouse droppings. The floor beneath it all
was once the discoteca municipal where Mami and Papi met
in another life. In this life the buildings aren't blown out, in this life
the American ammunition doesn't make it to the village, in this life
el paletero rings his bells to an audience of saplings.

Ritual for the Duende

Desde aquí se pueden escuchar las campanas que truenan en las montañas.
I write this on a postcard and send it first class to my antepasados.

I heard they were on life support but that they were getting better,
that they were looking forward to the day we'd escape the wound.

Notes

"Welcome to the Show"
The battle for Chavez Ravine refers to the decade-long resistance between generations of Mexican American families who were violently displaced by Los Angeles city officials for the construction of Dodger Stadium, also known as "Blue Heaven on Earth."

"How to Cook a Wolf"
This poem borrows its title and epigraph from the 1942 crisis cookbook by the food writer M. F. K. Fisher.

"Come, Little Hunger"
The lines "I've been told by people smarter than me that music puts out fire, / that the shower head doesn't carry all the voices you've ever heard" are indebted to the writers in Nabila Lovelace's Kenyon Review Young Writer's Workshop during the summer of 2023.

"Abandonarium (VI)"
The line "it's just a narrow bridge" is inspired by the Gloria Anzaldúa Altares Collection at UC Santa Cruz's Special Collections and Archives. Special thanks to the librarians at UC Santa Cruz and beyond who preserve radical, Queer, and feminist knowledges.

Acknowledgments

Friends, we get to hold this book in our hands because of everyone who held me along the way. It begins with the incredible patience of my teachers at the Los Angeles Unified School District; University of California, Irvine; the Writing MFA at Columbia University's School of the Arts; and the University of California, Santa Cruz's PhD in Literature and Creative/Critical Writing. I especially want to thank Susan Davis, Edward Victoria, Natalie Schonfeld, Timothy Donnelly, Mónica de la Torre, Susan Bernofsky, Natalie Diaz, Eduardo C. Corral, Oliver de la Paz, Evie Shockley, Edith Grossman, Deborah Paredez, Lucie Brock-Broido, Cynthia Cruz, Richard Howard, Mark Strand, Dorothea Lasky, Alan Gilbert, Seema Reza, Kendra Dority, Ronaldo V. Wilson, Chris Chen, Zac Zimmer, Amanda M. Smith, Micah Perks, Jennifer Tseng, Juan Poblete, and Lis Harris.

Gratitude to the editors of the publications in which these poems first appeared:

"English as a Second Language" *Boston Review's Poems for Political Disaster*; "Procession of Flies," *The Offing*; "Shelf Life," "The Last Town Before the Mojave," "Boys of Color," "The Mass Death of Mountains," "Altarpiece," and "Hymn for the Last Town," *The Last Town Before the Mojave* (Poetry Society of America); "Overtime" and "13 More American Landscapes, a View-Master Reel," *Frozen Sea*; "How to Cook a Wolf," "Come, Little Hunger," and "Empty Stadiums," *Shō Poetry Journal*; "Earthquake Weather," *McNeese Review*; and "Querida América" *Notre Dame Review*.

I am especially grateful to Shara McCallum, Alex Wolfe, Lesley Rains, and the rest of the editorial, production, and publicity team at University of Pittsburgh Press and the Pitt Poetry Series for believing in my work and helping me share it with others.

Thank you also to the Fine Arts Work Center, Kenyon Review's Young Writer's Workshop, and the Black Lawrence Press Manuscript Consultation Fellowship for providing me with precious attention, space, and time to tell these stories.

My deepest gratitude to my writing community and friends who inspired and encouraged me when I needed it the most. Thank you, Michael Gutierrez, Juan Moreno, Joshua Rocha, Mónica Moncada, Celeste Sandoval, Sherman Shi, Alex Han, Kunal Pathak, Anny Mogollón, Madison McCartha, Courtney Kersten, Carlos Cruz, Matthew Kelsey, Callista Buchen, Alex Bernstein, Nicholas Goodly, Chris Blackman, Michael Juliani, and everyone else who believed in these poems.

Thank you to my loving brothers and the rest of my thunderous family. Thank you, Ruben, Roxanna, Lucía, Julián, Abimael, Priscilla, Nicholas, Nick, Ter, and Dodger. Thank you, Sylmar. I hear you now and always.

Thank you to my querida Kristi, my sweetpea. Years ago, you let me start a crown of sonnets on your kitchen counter—with you everything became possible.

And thank you, always, Mami and Papi. Me diste el idioma, amor, y fuerza. For you two, it was always going to be a perfect game.